Copyright © 2020 Rainbow Books

All rights reserved. No part of this book may be reproduced, distributed or transmitted in any form or by any means, including photocoping, electronic or mechanical, recording or by any other form without written permission from the publisher.

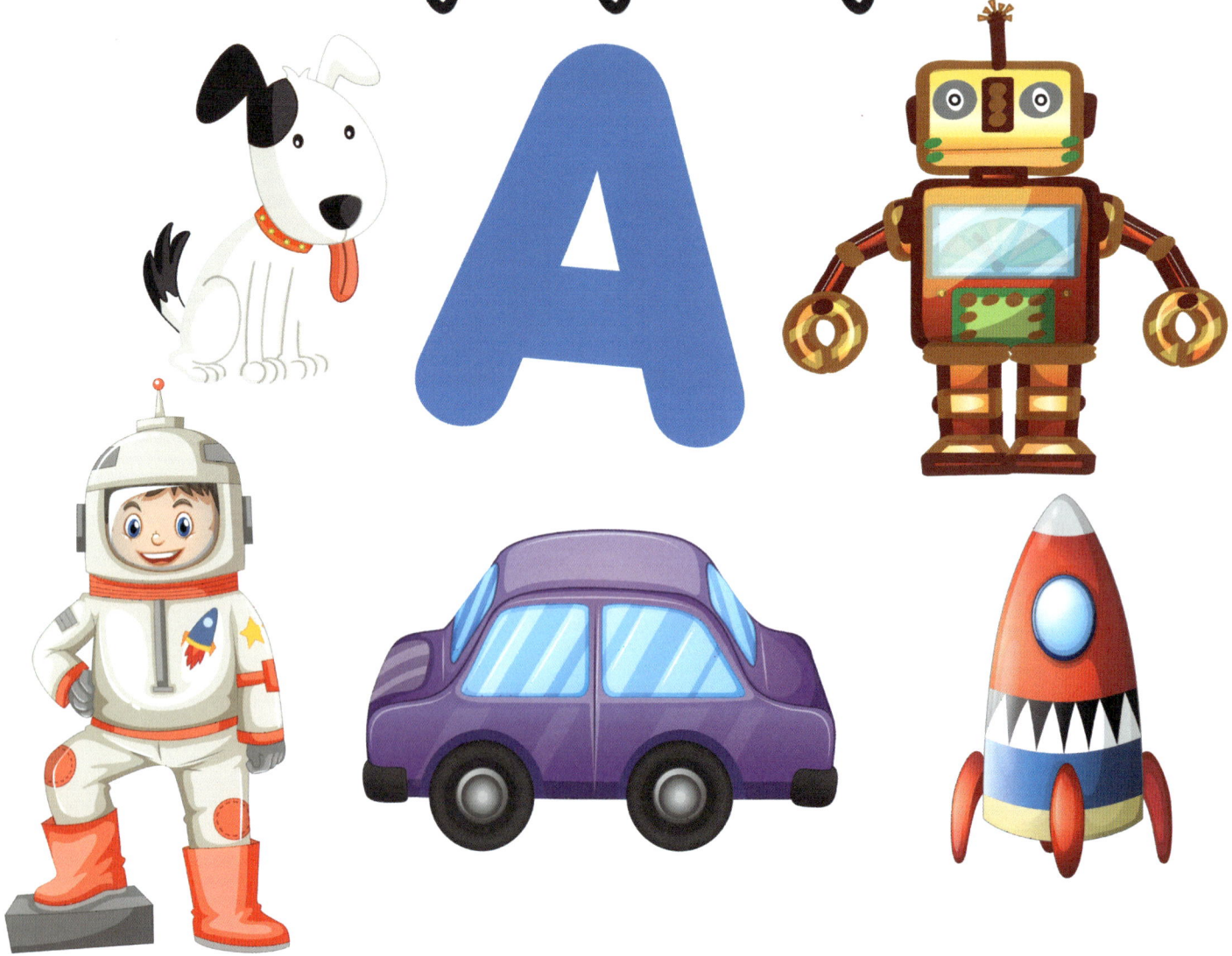

I SPY with my little eye something beginning with...

A

I SPY with my little eye something beginning with...

B

I SPY with my little eye something beginning with...

C

I SPY with my little eye something beginning with...

D

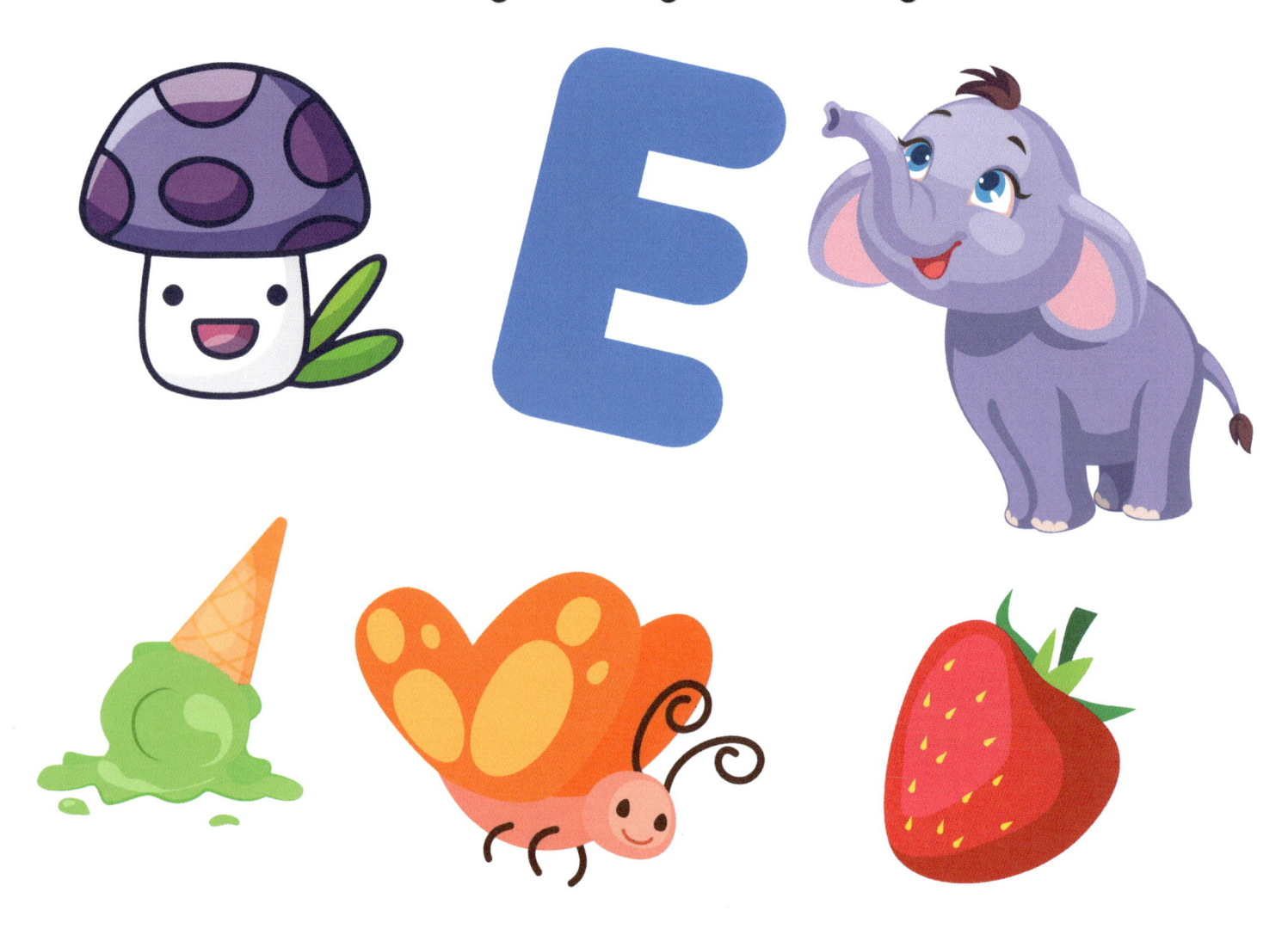

I SPY with my little eye something beginning with...

E

I SPY with my little eye something beginning with...

F

I SPY with my little eye something beginning with...

G

I SPY with my little eye something beginning with...

H

I SPY with my little eye something beginning with...

I SPY with my little eye something beginning with...

I SPY with my little eye something beginning with...

K

I SPY with my little eye something beginning with...

L

I SPY with my little eye something beginning with...

M

I SPY with my little eye something beginning with...

N

I SPY with my little eye something beginning with...

I SPY with my little eye something beginning with...

P

I SPY with my little eye something beginning with...

I SPY with my little eye something beginning with...

R

I SPY with my little eye something beginning with...

I SPY with my little eye something beginning with...

T

I SPY with my little eye something beginning with...

U

I SPY with my little eye something beginning with...

V

I SPY with my little eye something beginning with...

W

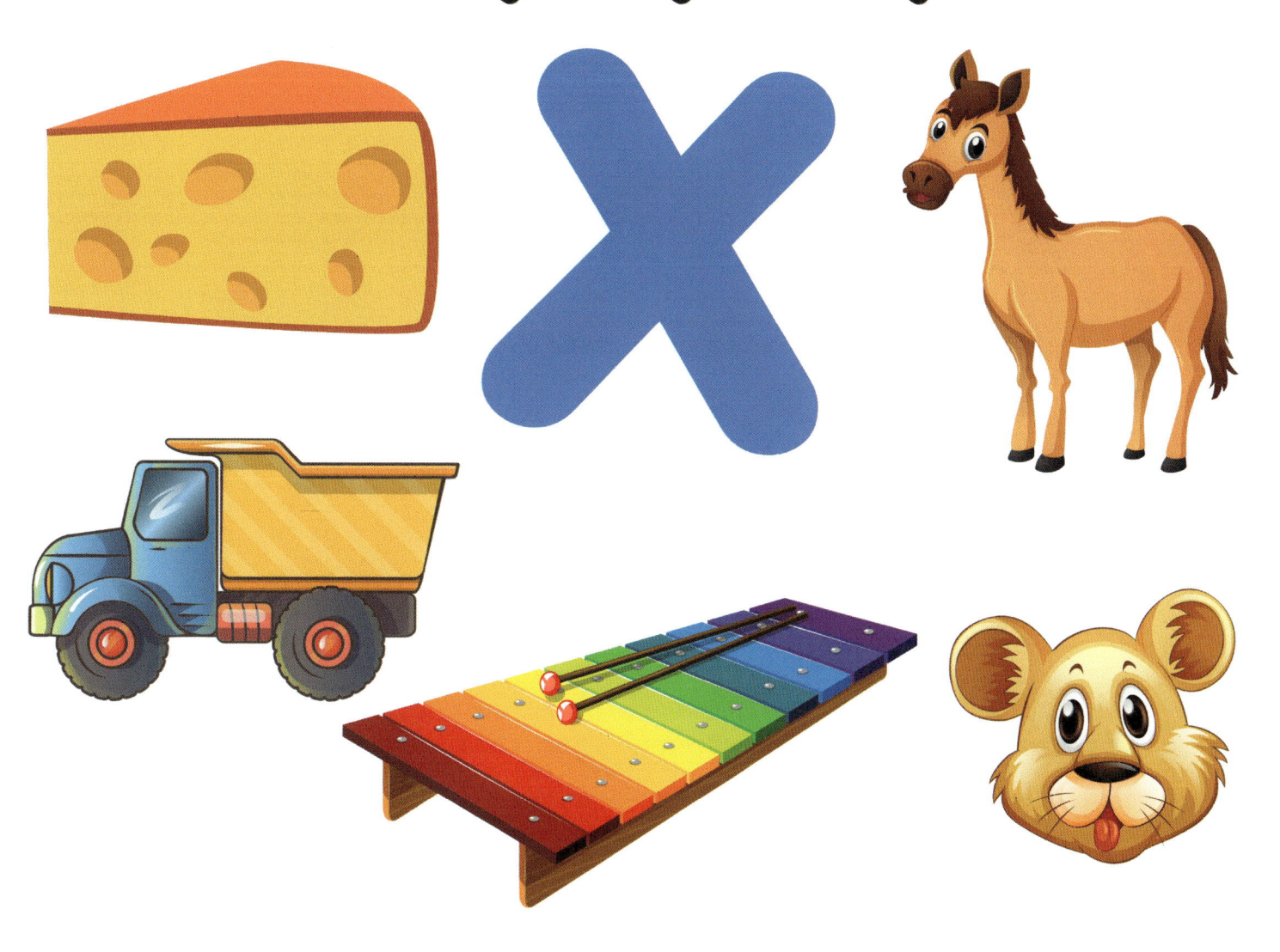

I SPY with my little eye something beginning with...

I SPY with my little eye something beginning with...

Y

I SPY with my little eye something beginning with...

z

A is for **Astronaut**

B is for **Bicycle**

C is for **Clown**

D is for **Dinosaur**

E is for **Elephant**

F is for **Fish**

G is for **Giraffe**

H is for **Hat**

I is for **Ice**

J is for **Joker**

K is for **Kid**

L is for **Lion**

M is for Money

N is for Nurse

O is for Octopus

P is for Panda

Q is for Question

R is for Rainbow

S is for Sun

T is for Train

U is for Money

V is for Vase

W is for Watermelon

X is for Xylophone

Y is for **Yoghurt**

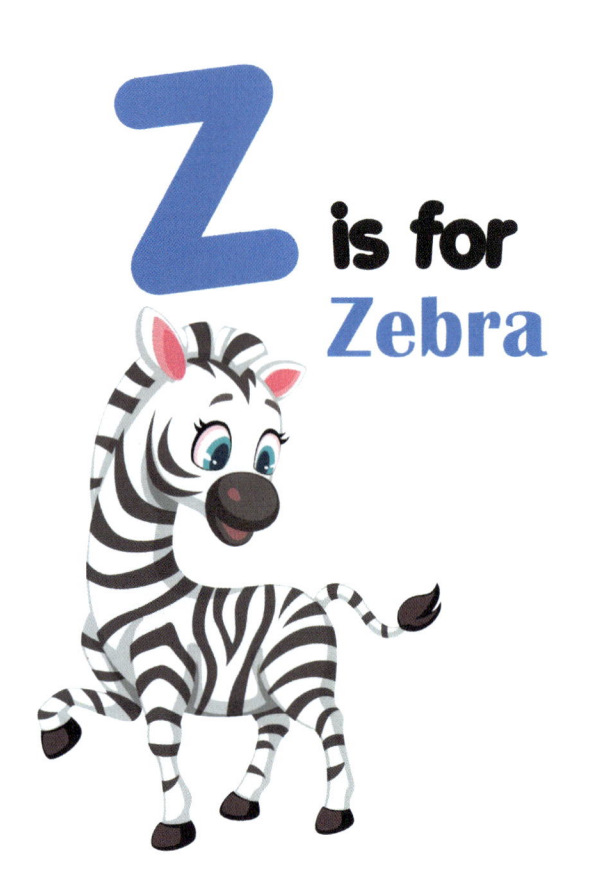

Z is for **Zebra**

Printed in Great Britain
by Amazon